CURRENT AND FUTURE CHALLENGES FOR ASIAN NONPROLIFERATION EXPORT CONTROLS: A REGIONAL RESPONSE

Scott A. Jones

October 2004

*****

The views expressed in this report are those of the author and do not necessarily reflect the official policy or position of the Department of the Army, the Department of Defense, or the U.S. Government. This report is cleared for public release; distribution is unlimited.

*****

Comments pertaining to this report are invited and should be forwarded to: Director, Strategic Studies Institute, U.S. Army War College, 122 Forbes Ave, Carlisle, PA 17013-5244. Copies of this report may be obtained from the Publications Office by calling (717) 245-4133, FAX (717) 245-3820, or by e-mail at *SSI_Publishing@carlisle.army.mil*

*****

All Strategic Studies Institute (SSI) monographs are available on the SSI Homepage for electronic dissemination. SSI's Homepage address is: *http://www.carlisle.army.mil/ssi/*

*****

The Strategic Studies Institute publishes a monthly e-mail newsletter to update the national security community on the research of our analysts, recent and forthcoming publications, and upcoming conferences sponsored by the Institute. Each newsletter also provides a strategic commentary by one of our research analysts. If you are interested in receiving this newsletter, please let us know by e-mail at *SSI_Newsletter@carlisle.army.mil* or by calling (717) 245-3133.

ISBN 1-58487-174-1

FOREWORD

The proliferation of weapons of mass destruction (WMD) and advanced conventional arms remains one of the gravest threats to the security of the international community. Countries of concern continue to pursue WMD by purchasing related technologies and components from foreign suppliers.

Export controls represent one of the key elements of a comprehensive nonproliferation strategy. They include procedures adopted by countries to regulate and monitor trade in weaponry and weapons-related (dual-use) technologies. However, the effectiveness of export control as a tool for limiting the spread of sensitive technologies and weaponry has been compromised by globalization and a complex array of international developments. The distinction between military and commercial products, for example, has become less clear. Therefore, it is likely that export control policies and institutions need to be continually adjusted if they are to serve international security objectives.

How countries in the Asia region respond to the relentlessly changing nature of the proliferation challenge will affect profoundly the shape of global security. In many instances, the countries of the region are major transshipment and assembly points for critical strategic dual-use goods and technologies. Some of these countries are major producers of strategic items, while others are or have potential to become suppliers. Yet, national export control systems in the region, with a few exceptions, remain rudimentary and resource-poor.

This monograph examines the current state of export control system development in the greater Asia region, with particular emphasis on the economic and security environment in which these systems operate. Identification then is made of the gains and remaining deficiencies in export control development. The monograph concludes by examining the applicability of the European Union's effort to coordinate export controls to the regional forces shaping the regional trade and security dynamics in Asia and what the United States can do to facilitate greater export control development and cooperation.

DOUGLAS C. LOVELACE, JR.
Director
Strategic Studies Institute

BIOGRAPHICAL SKETCH OF THE AUTHOR

SCOTT A. JONES is Director of Export Control Programs at the Center for International Trade and Security at The University of Georgia. Upon completing his MA, Dr. Jones took a year-long position at the Delegation of the Commission for the European Union (EU) in Washington, DC. Subsequently, Mr. Jones worked for Los Alamos National Laboratory on a Department of Energy/ Los Alamos program that assisted the former Soviet Republics in export control development. His areas of specialization include foreign and security policy of the states of the former Soviet Union, Ukraine, export control developments in the EU, and conventional arms transfers. In addition, he has briefed government officials from Russia, Ukraine, the Caucasus states, the United States, and Europe on export control and security-related issues. He has received research and travel grants from the United States Institute of Peace, the National Research Council, the W. Alton Jones Foundation, and other foundations. Dr. Jones is the author of *The Evolution of the Ukrainian Export Control System: State Building and International Cooperation* (London: Ashgate, 2002). He is also a contributor to *Arms on the Market: Reducing the Risk of Proliferation in the Former Soviet Union* (New York: Routledge Press, 1998) and a co-editor of and contributor to *Crossroads and Conflict: Security and Foreign Policy in the Caucasus and Central Asia* (New York: Routledge Press, 1999). He has published articles in *Arms Exports* (in Russian), *The Middle East Review, Contemporary Security Policy, Defense News, Jane's Intelligence Review, East Asian Review, The Nonproliferation Review,* and *The Monitor: International Perspectives on Nonproliferation Nuclear Control* (in Russian). Dr. Jones received his BA and Ph.D. in political science and philosophy at the University of Georgia and a MA at Lancaster University in the UK.

SUMMARY

As recent investigations into the vast nuclear network fronted by Pakistani scientist A. Q. Khan have made clear, the black market in nuclear supplies operated with ease and impunity. Much of this network was located and operated in Malaysia, a country with, at best, a rudimentary export control system. Through normal trade channels, the constituent components of nuclear weapons originated in and transited through this Asian nation, serving to draw further attention to how states in this economically dynamic region oversee the trade in strategic goods and technologies.

Export controls represent one of the key elements of a comprehensive nonproliferation strategy. They include procedures adopted by countries to regulate and monitor trade in weaponry and weapons-related (dual-use) technologies. However, the effectiveness of export control as a tool for limiting the spread of sensitive technologies and weaponry has been compromised by globalization and a complex array of international developments. The distinction between military and commercial products, for example, has become less clear. Therefore, it is likely that export control policies and institutions need to be continually adjusted if they are to serve international security objectives.

Regional export control standards are quite varied. For example, over the past 2 years, China passed legislation related to nuclear, chemical and biological, missile, and military exports. Taiwan updated its export regulations with regards to Mainland trade. South Korea implemented a catch-all regulation. And Singapore passed legislation strengthening state control over the export of strategic goods, including munitions and related dual-use goods. Other states, such as Laos, Myanmar, and Malaysia, have made only minor, primarily legislative, changes, most of which are superficial. For example, despite U.S. efforts to persuade Malaysia to adopt more stringent nuclear export controls, its foreign minister said that he did not currently "see any necessity" to sign the Additional Protocol to Malaysia's nuclear safeguards agreement. Recent disclosures about Libya's nuclear program revealed that a Malaysian firm manufactured some of Tripoli's nuclear equipment.

How countries in the Asia region respond to the relentlessly changing nature of the proliferation challenge will affect profoundly the shape of global security for many years. In many instances, the countries of the region are major transshipment and assembly points for critical strategic dual-use goods and technologies. Some of these countries are already major producers of strategic items, while others are or have potential to become suppliers. Yet, national export control systems in the region, with a few exceptions, remain rudimentary and resource-poor.

As Asia develops into a clearly demarcated economic "region," it is confronted by similar export control challenges as those faced in Europe with the advent of the Common Market. As such, a regional system of export control standards and practices emerged as a means to ensure not only economic parity, but regional and international security as well. While not necessarily as advanced in terms of regional identity as the European free trade area, the states of Asia could benefit profitably from a regional approach to export control development and coordination.

In addition, the states of Asia could also gain from increased export control cooperation with the United States. As a global leader in nonproliferation, the United States can provide critical assistance to export control development efforts through training and the allocation of other resources. Likewise, the United States should focus its export control outreach efforts to the less developed export control systems in Asia, especially the transshipment countries.

The intersection of trade and security cuts to the heart of the matter in Asia, where national economies profoundly depend on trade, as they do on regional and international security. The internal challenge for countries of the Asia region is to develop systems compatible with their political, economic, and security needs, while addressing the overall threat posed by the proliferation of weapons of mass destruction.

CURRENT AND FUTURE CHALLENGES FOR ASIAN NONPROLIFERATION EXPORT CONTROLS: A REGIONAL RESPONSE

INTRODUCTION

The proliferation of weapons of mass destruction (WMD) and advanced conventional arms remains one of the gravest threats to the security of the international community. Countries of concern continue to pursue WMD by purchasing related technologies and components from foreign suppliers. Recent disclosures regarding the extent of Pakistan's involvement in nuclear proliferation suggest the security ramifications of international trade remain vital concerns. Of increasing alarm, too, is the tangible threat posed by terrorist organizations such as al-Qaeda that are seeking to inflict mass casualties, a fact in keeping with the increasing lethality of international terrorism.[1] Furthermore, unregulated arms transfers can introduce instability and conflict into countries and regions, making them breeding grounds for terrorism.

A great deal of policy attention and resources has been directed towards addressing this proliferation threat, as well as towards securing nuclear materials from possible theft or sabotage. Nevertheless, policymakers should not overlook that most countries and terrorists seek to *purchase* the components they need for developing WMD.[2] Consequently, greater attention and resources need to be devoted to strengthening export controls, with consideration for the needs of legitimate trade.

Export controls represent one of the key elements of a comprehensive nonproliferation strategy. They include procedures adopted by countries to regulate and monitor trade in weaponry and weapons-related (dual-use) technologies. However, the effectiveness of export control as a tool for limiting the spread of sensitive technologies and weaponry has been compromised by globalization and a complex array of international developments. The distinction between military and commercial products, for example, has become less clear.[3] Therefore, it is likely that export control policies and institutions need to be adjusted continually if they are to serve international security objectives.

How countries in the Asia region respond to the relentlessly changing nature of the proliferation challenge will affect profoundly the shape of global security for many years.[4] In many instances, the countries of the region are major transshipment and assembly points for critical strategic dual-use goods and technologies.[5] Some of these countries are already major producers of strategic items, while others are or have potential to become suppliers.[6] Yet, national export control systems in the region, with a few exceptions, remain rudimentary and resource-poor.[7]

This monograph examines the current state of export control system development in the greater Asia region, with particular emphasis on the economic and security environment in which these systems operate. Identification is then made of the gains and remaining deficiencies in export control development. The author concludes by examining the applicability of the European Union's effort to coordinate export controls to the regional forces shaping the trade and security dynamics in Asia.

THE ECONOMIC CONTEXT: GREATER REGIONALIZATION AND INTERDEPENDENCE

Increasing regionalization—regionalization being the complex network of flows across state boundaries involving the movement of goods and services, capital, technology, information, and people—best characterizes the Asian economic context.[8] Intra-Asian trade accounts for about 45 percent of East Asia's total trade. In addition, trade throughput via and from the region has increased dramatically since the late 1960s.[9] For example, 11 of the top 20 "megaports" are in Asia (see Table 1).[10]

1. **Hong Kong**	8. **Tokyo**	15. La Spezia
2. **Shanghai**	9. Genoa	16. Felixstowe
3. **Singapore**	10. **Yantian**	17. Algeciras
4. **Kaohsiung**	11. Antwerp	18. **Kobe**
5. Rotterdam	12. **Nagoya**	19. **Yokohama**
6. **Pusan**	13. Le Havre	20. **Laem Chabang**
7. Bremerhaven	14. Hamburg	

* Bold indicates ports in Asia.

Table 1. World Megaports.

Between 1990 and 2001, Asia's share of global merchandise and commercial services exports rose from 21.8 percent to 25 percent, and 16.8 percent to 20.8 percent, respectively. During the same period, the comparable share for the Association of South East Asian Nations (ASEAN) countries rose from 4.2 percent to 6.4 percent. The Chinese share of global exports rose from 1.8 percent to 4.4 percent.[11] In the case of China, the last few years have seen much higher levels of economic interaction with the rest of Asia. Sino-Japanese trade reached U.S.$53.9 billion in 2002, and exports from China to Japan increased by 3.1 percent to U.S.$25.7 billion and imports from Japan rose 14.5 percent to U.S.$28.2 billion. Japan is now China's second largest trading partner, while China became the largest importer of Japanese goods and services in the first half of 2002. Hong Kong, Taiwan, South Korea, Singapore, and Thailand are also among China's top 10 trading partners. Taiwan is China's fifth-largest trading partner. Since 1987, trade between mainland China and Taiwan has totaled almost $2 trillion; it grew at a 7 percent annual rate in 1999.[12]

The regional concentration of trade is but one of several indicators of regionalization. Underlying much of the rapid expansion of intraregional trade in recent years has been a massive expansion in foreign direct investment (FDI) flows in the region. Trade policy reform has figured prominently in the rising importance of trade and FDI in the region. Unilateral liberalization of tariff and nontariff barriers took place in Indonesia, Malaysia, the Republic of Korea, and Thailand during the 1990s.[13] The accelerated relocation of Japanese production in different parts of Asia has been particularly significant. It has established Japan as the undisputed leader in Asia in terms of technology transfer, capital goods, and economic aid.[14] Having achieved a secure foothold in Korea and Taiwan, Japan has since rapidly expanded its stake in the ASEAN economies, and is developing a substantial presence in China and Indochina. The relocation and off-shore model of production ensures a greater diffusion of technology.

The interpenetration of national economies is also stimulated by the exponential growth of financial flows across national boundaries, coupled with the increasing dominance of intra-company as a proportion of bilateral trade. The degree of financial interdependence was evidenced by the 1997 financial crisis, which resulted in the Chiang Mai + 3 Initiative.[15] Intra-company trade currently accounts for nearly four-fifths of Japan's total exports and half of its imports. Complementing and reinforcing these transnational production structures is the emergence of such regional economic zones as the Johor-Singapore-Riau Growth Triangle, the Indonesia-Malaysia-Thailand Growth Triangle, the East Asia Growth Area, the Southern China Growth Triangle, and the Tumen River Delta Economic.[16] Finally, mention must be made of the increasing mobility of labor, with the strongly performing economies of the region attracting large numbers of legal and illegal immigrants, some of whom may have links to terrorist organizations.[17]

Energy sharing has been one of the most notable examples of regional cooperation. In January 2001, the leaders of Indonesia and Singapore opened a vital underwater gas pipeline between their nations. During the next 20 years, this pipeline is expected to channel more than $8 billion worth of natural gas from Indonesia's West Natuna fields to Singapore. Because wealthy Singapore has virtually no natural resources, Indonesia viewed its natural gas and other resources as tools to be used for political gain. Thus the pipeline was a sizable accomplishment, reflecting an increasing maturity in the political relationship between the two countries. Other gas deals are in development. Malaysia plans to build a pipeline to West Natuna and is encouraging Bangkok to develop gas fields in the Gulf of Thailand. Similarly, Thailand and Burma have begun extracting gas from eastern Burma's Yadana deposits.[18] China's expanding economy will also require vast infusions of foreign energy, likely prompting Beijing to attempt to tap into Southeast Asia's gas fields. Meanwhile, in Northeast Asia, Japan has inked several deals to purchase the majority of Brunei's oil.[19]

Nevertheless, the extent, intensity, and efficiency of these economic and functional linkages are clearly limited.[20] There are many states (Cambodia, Laos, North Korea, and several of the Pacific island states) and many areas within states (e.g., noncoastal areas of China, parts of Burma, and the Russian Far East), where these linkages are nonexistent or at best tenuous. Moreover, many of the linkages which are said to contribute to regional interdependence (e.g., Japan-ASEAN trade and investment flows) are acutely asymmetrical, and, to that extent, likely to promote social and political tensions both within and across national boundaries. Nevertheless, both the continuing intermingling of economies and trade flows and interdependence of financial systems define—and to some extent delimit—the scope of the "Asian" region in a manner that transcends the traditional boundaries of states.[21]

THE SECURITY CONTEXT: MILITARIZATION AND PROLIFERATION

During the last decade, the top three regions for arms imports—Western Europe, the Middle East, and East Asia—accounted for 78 percent of the world's arms imports. Of the top five arms importing countries in 2000, two are in East Asia—Japan and Taiwan. Military spending, armed forces, and arms acquisition are all rising in Asia. Between 1988 and 1998, as global military expenditures fell by 35 percent, those in East Asia and the Pacific actually increased by 38 percent. (South Asia increased its military spending by 25 percent.) Figures from the Stockholm International Peace Research Institute note that military expenditures declined worldwide from $1.066 trillion in 1988 to $719 billion in 1998. But in Asia, they climbed from $95 billion to $130 billion.

Japan, China, and the Koreas have accounted for the majority of the region's military spending during the past decade, while the arms race between India and Pakistan has swelled South Asia's military budgets. Less visibly, military expenditures in ASEAN countries increased by 52 percent in real terms between 1988 and 1997. This increase, greater in both absolute and percentage terms than that of any other region, occurred as the world as a whole cut military spending by more than one-third (see Table 2).[22]

The increased spending is going, in large part, to the acquisition of technologically advanced conventional weapon systems: combat aircraft, ocean-going naval ships, tanks, armored vehicles, armed helicopters, and missiles and related dual-use components and technologies.[23] Moreover, much new acquisition is through domestic

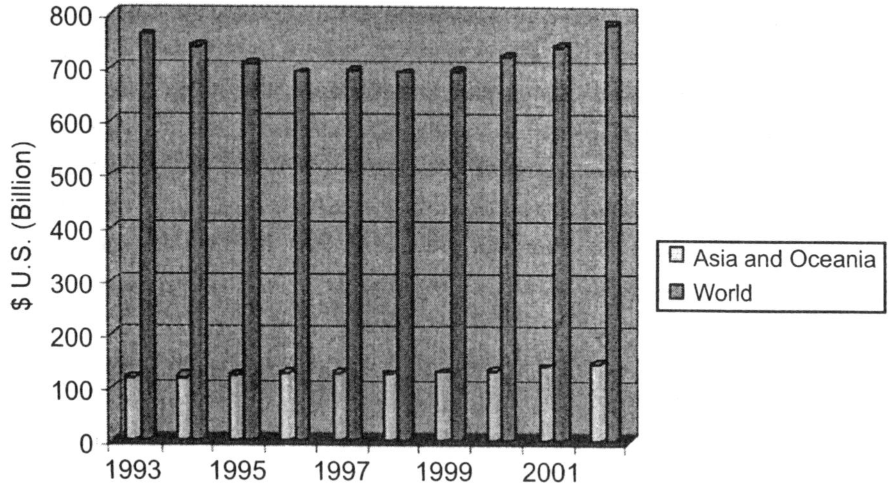

Table 2. Military Expenditure (1993-2002).

arms production. China, Japan, South Korea, India, and Taiwan are pursuing the development of national arms industries that could eventually make them, in theory, fully independent of foreign imports.[24]

Proliferation continues to pose a particular threat to the security and stability of East Asia, where several states already have nuclear weapons and ballistic missile capabilities, and others have the technical expertise necessary to develop WMD.[25] For example, the U.S. Central Intelligence Agency contends that throughout the second half of 2001, North Korea continued to export significant ballistic missile-related equipment, components, materials, and technical expertise to the Middle East, South Asia, and North Africa.[26] P'yongyang attaches high priority to the development and sale of ballistic missiles, equipment, and related technology.[27] Exports of ballistic missiles and related technology are one of the North's major sources of hard currency, which fuel continued missile development and production.[28] In addition, in a provocative decision, North Korea announced on December 12, 2002, that it was restarting nuclear facilities that had been frozen since 1994, and it ordered international monitors to leave the country. As international concern grew that P'yongyang was resuming its nuclear weapons program, North Korea announced January 10, 2003, that it was immediately withdrawing from the nuclear Nonproliferation Treaty (NPT). Shortly thereafter, it began a series of provocative missile tests, culminating in a test during the inauguration of South Korea's new president.[29] In addition, many North Korean trading companies in Southeast Asia—mainly in Thailand, Singapore and Hong Kong—have been set up with the specific purpose of obtaining technology for North Korea's defense industries (for more in-depth case study, see Appendix I).[30]

For its part, Beijing has taken steps to address U.S. and other concerns and increase its partial participation in international nonproliferation regimes since 1991.[31] Nevertheless, for much of the 1990s, China's proliferation record was poor. For example, the Director of Central Intelligence (DCI) noted that, for July-December 1996, "China was the most significant supplier of WMD-related goods and technology to foreign countries."[32] The 1998 report of the Rumsfeld Commission identified China's weapons proliferation as a "threat." The DCI's semi-annual reports have named the People's Republic of China (PRC) (plus Russia and North Korea) as "key suppliers" of dangerous technology.[33] Although Chinese firms continue to provide some worrisome dual-use assistance to a few countries (such as Pakistan and Iran), the scope, content, and frequency of its export of sensitive weapons-related items has declined and diminished. In the latter half of the 1990s, the Chinese government began to institutionalize its nonproliferation commitments by developing its export control infrastructure, a trend that has continued in recent years. Moreover, an expanding community of Chinese officials, scientists, military officers, and academics involved in arms control and nonproliferation research and policymaking has helped sensitize senior leaders to the importance of these issues to the country's overall foreign policy and national security.[34] China recently gained membership in the Nuclear Suppliers Group (NSG), and has expressed similar interest in joining the Missile Technology Control Regime.[35]

Finally is the looming threat of terrorism. For example, in a recent report on the threat of terrorism in South East Asia, the government of Singapore said that, while some of these groups existed before al-Qaeda and have local agendas, their link-up with Osama bin Laden's organization had made them more deadly. The report further noted that although the U.S.-led military strikes on Afghanistan had disrupted al-Qaeda bases, bin Laden's network could still tap alliances in Asia, including Jemaah Islamiah, to stage more attacks: "With their radical agenda and their enhanced skills acquired from al-Qaeda, these groups, if left unchecked, will pose a grave threat to the security of South-East Asia for a long time to come."[36]

In summary, growing trade interdependence, increasing indigenous design and production capabilities (i.e., a growing pool of potential and actual sensitive technologies suppliers), expanding military budgets, intensified technology transfers to and from the region, and an ever-expanding share of the cargo trade market represent the regional challenges to the configuration and effective execution of nonproliferation export controls.

At the global level, governments are also confronted with several obstacles to practicing effective export controls. Globalization presents several challenges, such as the transnationalization of the defense industry, the rapidly blurring distinction between civilian and military technologies, the increasing intangibility of technology and its transference, and the incessant need to update control lists because of the brisk turnovers in technological developments. The mercurial threat of terrorist use of WMD amplifies these difficulties.[37]

Overall, the abiding export controls challenge for any government is identifying, then striking, the proper balance between trade and security. The very name of this nonproliferation tool is imprecise—export *control*—with the connotation being that trade comes at the expense of security. The nexus of trade and security cuts to the heart of the matter in Asia, where national economies profoundly depend on trade, as they do on regional and international security. The internal challenge for countries of the Asia region is to develop systems compatible with their political, economic, and security needs while addressing the overall threat posed by the proliferation of WMD. The next section examines the gains made by and deficiencies in the nonproliferation export control systems of the Asian region.

CURRENT ASIAN EXPORT CONTROL DEVELOPMENT: GAINS AND DEFICIENCIES

In terms of export control development, the Asian region represents a wide array of stages. However, one of the most significant characteristics of export control policies in East Asia is the strong correlation between levels of economic growth and implementation of multilateral export control measures; that is, a country that started economic growth in an earlier period and has a high gross domestic product (GDP) level tends to implement more complete measures of export controls.[38] For example, Japan has one of the most sophisticated export control systems in the world.[39] Japan has also been active in nonproliferation export control regimes, having been a founding member the Australia Group, the Missile Technology Control Regime (MTCR), the NSG, and the Wassenaar Arrangment.

In addition, the Japanese government has played a key leadership role in regional nonproliferation export controls by establishing basic guidelines that include nonproliferation factors in providing official development assistance (e.g., Official Development Assistance [ODA] Charter implemented in 1991)[40] and by disseminating information on export controls through multilateral seminars (e.g., Asian Export Control Seminar started in 1993), bilateral talks, and training programs.[41] In 1994, Japan also introduced a General Bulk License comparable to similar procedures in the United States and Europe. The procedure rewards Japanese trading partners for setting up export control programs by simplifying and shortening licensing procedures. In the region, Hong Kong (April 1994) and South Korea (October 1994) were the first to receive this status. Since more than 64 percent of Japanese exports of the items formerly controlled by the Coordinating Committee on Multilateral Export Controls (COCOM) go to countries in the region, all of which require licenses, the Japanese government hopes this will help induce more of its regional neighbors to adopt complementary export control systems.[42] For example, Japan received a South Korean task force team of export control officials in September 2002 to assist with the introduction of catch-all controls in Republic of Korea (ROK). Other recent bilateral initiatives include bilateral agreements signed with

Hong Kong and Singapore aimed at preventing indirect exports of products that can be converted into weapons.[43]

In other states of the region, export control developments varied in 2002. For example, China passed a raft of legislation related to nuclear, chemical and biological, missile, and military exports.[44] Taiwan updated its export regulations with regard to Mainland trade. South Korea implemented a catch-all regulation, and Singapore passed legislation strengthening state control over the export of strategic goods, including munitions and related dual-use goods.[45] Other states, such as Laos, Myanmar, and Malaysia, have made only minor, primarily legislative, changes, most of which are superficial. For example, despite U.S. efforts to persuade Malaysia to adopt more stringent nuclear export controls, its foreign minister said that he did not currently "see any necessity" to sign the Additional Protocol to Malaysia's nuclear safeguards agreement. Recent disclosures about Libya's nuclear program revealed that a Malaysian firm manufactured some of Tripoli's nuclear equipment.[46]

While other control systems in the region may not be as comprehensive as Japan's, it is important to consider that individual economic and political profiles are relevant to the form of the export control system. To use the Japanese example again, Japan is a key supplier country, a major economic and political power, as well as a transshipment point. Comprehensive licensing, enforcement, and regime adherence elements are appropriate to its political and economic particulars. Mongolia, on the other hand, is not a supplier country and therefore may not have comprehensive end-use checks or extensive government outreach functions in place. Indonesia, furthermore, lists only one industry—P. T. Pindad—as exporting controlled goods and technologies and therefore does not require a significant industry outreach capacity. Nevertheless, while the forms may vary, there must be a higher degree of harmonization between states of the region to ensure that loopholes are not exploited. To that end, three critical areas requiring further attention remain.[47]

Technology Controls and Control List Harmonization.

The vast majority of Asian countries still do not have adequate technology controls in place. With only Japan and South Korea being members of the multilateral export control arrangements, coordinating national export control systems with international norms is a problem. For example, as of late 2001, 7 out of 17 countries had no or only partial controls over the export or transit of sensitive technologies.[48] One country does not have controls on items from any of the multilateral lists, while another does not control goods on the NSG and Australia Group lists. A third country has no legal controls on dual-use equipment that could be used for chemical weapons (CW) and biological weapons (BW). Finally, while another maintains no formal controls on the items on the Chemical Weapons Convention (CWC) schedules or on biological weapons, it does control CW- and BW-related dual-use equipment. Furthermore, the majority of surveyed countries lack national control lists that reflect those of the four multilateral export control regimes. However, a few countries, such as Singapore, are in the process of harmonizing their control lists (see Table 3).

	Goods		**Technology**
	Arms, Nuclear/ BCW Missile Related item	Dual-use items	
Brunei	Yes	Yes	No
Cambodia	Yes	Partial	No
China	Yes	Partial	Yes
Hong Kong, China	Yes	Yes	Yes
Indonesia	Partial	Partial	No
Japan	Yes	Yes	Yes
Korea	Yes	Yes	Yes
Laos	Partial	Partial	Yes
Macau, China	Yes	Yes	Yes
Malaysia	Partial	Partial	No
Mongolia	Partial	Partial	Partial
Myanmar	Yes	Partial	Partial
Philippines	Partial	No	No
Singapore	Partial	Partial	No
Chinese Taipei	Yes	Partial	Partial
Thailand	Yes	Partial	Yes
Viet Nam	Yes	Partial	Partial

Table 3. Scope of Control, 2002.

While an important exercise, the harmonization of national control lists for regime nonmembers need not be an exacting process. An emerging trend in the practice of export controls is the move to so-called "activity-based" controls from the purely control list approach.[49]

1. The control-list approach focuses on the nature of the product or technology itself, and regulates export through product control lists. Typically, under this approach, an exporter first determines whether its product is covered by the product list and, if so, then consults the product list to determine what restrictions, if any, apply to the export of the product.
2. The activity-based approach, by contrast, focuses on the nature of the transaction and the identity of the exporter and its partners in the deal. It is *not* limited to an examination of the specific product being shipped. The purpose of an activity-based approach is to control certain dangerous activities, such as the proliferation of nuclear or chemical weapons or the advancement of terrorist organizations.

As the nature of the proliferation threat becomes geographically boundless, the role of activity-based controls has become increasingly significant as a mechanism for enforcing export control policy. Studies have indicated that proliferant countries often seek threshold or decontrolled technology for their WMD programs.[50] Furthermore, the events of September 11, 2001, have accelerated this changing trend in, for example, U.S. export control legislation. The "bad guys" are no longer limited to a particular country.[51] As a result, all transactions, even those that seem purely domestic, and transactions in "friendly countries," now fall under the scope of export control laws. Countries, therefore, must have the ability to control exports irrespective of list content. This flexibility has otherwise caused a catch-all clause, a tool not readily in abundance in the Asian region.

Catch-All Controls.

National control systems focus on the end-use and end-user of goods and technologies, allowing more freedom to transfer dual-use technologies to commercial end-users for commercial end-uses. Post-Gulf War disclosures of the operational means of Iraqi front companies furthered the spread of catch-all. Heightened concerns over terrorist acquisition of WMD components and technologies highlight the preventative role offered by catch-all legislation.

A "catch-all" regulation is the means by which governments apply existing national export control procedures to goods and technologies not on national control lists when it is known or suspected that such goods of technologies will be used in WMD programs. This type of regulation is also known as "end use" regulation, because it requires that exporters ensure that their exports of dual-use products have legitimate end uses.[52]

Japan, for example, amended two cabinet orders to introduce a catch-all control in December 2001. The new regulation came into force in April 2002. Under the new control, the export of items which are not included in the export control list requires export license of the items that are for use in connection with WMD and their delivery means. To ensure the effectiveness of the catch-all clause, the Ministry of Economy, Trade and Industry (METI) provides exporters the "End User List" that indicates end users of proliferation concern. South Korea also enacted a catch-all clause in early 2003.

With respect to China, officials believe they have the authority and already have implemented catch-all controls for several kinds of nonproliferation items. Moreover, the Ministry of Foreign Trade and Economic Cooperation (MOFTEC) can restrict both nuclear and nuclear dual-use items that do not appear on the list.[53] Allegedly, officials also interpret catch-all controls to permit restrictions on e-mail and fax transfers of technology. Officials indicate, however, that they need assistance in devising means to control these intangible forms of technology transfer effectively. In contrast, at least one source claimed that the government must put chemical items on the list before they can exercise controls, although the regulations would then allow officials to restrict a host of associated production equipment and technologies. Although the central government appears to have the authority to use catch-all controls, the process for implementing these controls seems ambiguous.[54]

Apart from Japan and South Korea, the majority of reporting Asian states either lack completely or do not have multilateral export control regime standard catch-all control regulations. This characteristic is further reinforced by the relative absence of information that regional governments provide their exporters and transportation industries on end users and entities of concern. With the exception of a few countries, regional governments—to the extent they provide any export control-related information—share only the minimal amount of information, usually pertaining to compliance requirements. The functional essence of the catch-all regulation is a greater responsibility on behalf of industry to ensure that end use and end user are in no way illicit. Yet, industry must be adequately informed.

Reexport and Transshipment Controls.

Another way to maximize the ability to administer and enforce export controls is to focus international monitoring and enforcement efforts on major chokepoints in the flow of global commerce. A significant amount of global trade passes through a handful of major transshipment hubs—most of which are in the Asia region—that serve as key distribution points in the global economy. For example, the equivalent of more than 50 million containers a year has passed through the major ports of Southeast Asia in recent years.[55]

Such hubs potentially could be used by terrorists or countries of concern to divert sensitive items to unauthorized destinations or end users. Tighter national export controls and greater international cooperation have made direct access to items more difficult for end users of proliferation concern. Proliferators increasingly are likely to use transit points in unsuspecting destinations to conceal the real nature of the transaction. They falsify cargo descriptions, do not enter end-user/user destinations, hide the final destination, use front companies, and try other ruses.[56]

Most of the countries surveyed do not have legislation covering re-exports or transshipment controls. This relative deficiency is perhaps the most serious export control challenge, in light of the fact that most countries are—in proliferation terms—not suppliers but transshipment points, whose economies depend on the efficiencies and speed of trade facilitation. Compounding matters is the relative proximity of key technology suppliers, such as Japan and South

Korea.[57] For example, according to a Tokyo Metropolitan Police Department press release, authorities arrested the former managing director of the Ryokasha Company and Hitachi for conspiring to sell telecomparators to China.[58] The sale of telecomparators is in violation of a Japanese law established by the Nuclear Suppliers Group in 1992. This device can be modified to develop an apparatus for the extraction of weapons grade plutonium. The company allegedly used South Korea as a transshipment point to avoid Japanese export controls to its final destination in Harbin, China. According to the police investigation, 3 months after 18 telecomparators were shipped to Harbin in December 1996, the Ryokosha company sent technicians to offer assistance and to repair the products.[59]

Another case involved Singapore as a transshipment point. In May 2001, U.S. Customs Special Agents in Baltimore initiated an investigation based on a referral made by the Defense Security Service which alleged that a U.S. national was attempting to acquire sophisticated encryption technology and related data for illegal export to the PRC. The technology is controlled for export under the U.S. Munitions List of the International Trafficking in Arms Regulations and by the National Security Agency. Based on the referral, an undercover investigation was initiated, and the perpetrators were arrested for attempting to unlawfully export the encryption devices to the PRC via Singapore.[60]

Addressing the 2002 Southeast Asian regional forum on transshipment controls in Bangkok, the State Department's Bureau of Nonproliferation, Director of the Office of Export Control Cooperation John Schlosser, remarked:

> State sponsors of terrorism and terrorist organizations increasingly are attempting to exploit the less-stringent controls that exist in the world's transshipment hubs—often by diverting legitimate trade or through front companies posing as honest brokers. Unless transshipment countries—like those you represent here today—catch up with these supplier states and similarly strengthen their export control systems, they will remain an attractive target for this kind of predatory trade.[61]

With notable exceptions, the export control systems of Asia are resource poor. While overall progress in export control development is evident, individual discrepancies continue to pose threats to regional and international security.[62] As noted above, increasing economic integration and interdependence creates a natural base upon which to develop regional export control resources and greater coordination, although, until 1997, the region was slow to pursue collective responses to regional public goods problems.

A REGIONAL RESPONSE: THE EUROPEAN UNION CASE AS MODEL

Export controls combine trade and security policy; to this extent, regional economic integration and harmonization presume some degree of security policy cooperation. An instructive model for future regional export control developments is the European Union (EU).[63]

As a consequence of increasingly harmonized trade policy, the EU eventually addressed the issue of a common framework for the export of dual-use and goods and technologies from the community in the 1990s. Presently, the 15 member states operate under a common control list and set of export guidelines (e.g., such as an EU-level catch-all clause requirement), recognize a common license, regularly share licensing and enforcement information, and are subject to compliance reviews. In addition, until the year 2000, an EU member state easily could grant an export license for an item for which the authorities of another member state had refused authorization. Under a new regulation, such undercutting can provoke considerable peer pressure. Member states now have to 1) inform each other on denials of export licenses; 2) consult with each other on their intention to undercut; and, 3) explain their decision to do so.[64] The EU is also coordinating members state export control assistance to the 10 inductees.

In Asia, the concept of "comprehensive" or "integrated" security, which would include nonproliferation export control efforts, initially was championed by Japan in the late 1970s.[65] It was developed further by ASEAN in the 1980s. In the 1990s, when China made increasing use of the concept, it gained even wider currency throughout Asia. Throughout most of the Asia region, the Asian financial crisis of 1997 has reinforced further the belief that security must be understood in "comprehensive" terms that go beyond traditional military connotations.[66] Similarly, the regional terrorist threat has galvanized calls for regional threat management.[67]

ASEAN, established initially as a trade and development forum, has, in fact, sought to coordinate regional nonproliferation efforts. ASEAN has hosted seminars on nonproliferation and initiated the 1995 Treaty on the Southeast Asia Nuclear Weapons-Free Zone (Bangkok Treaty). Recently, Japanese trade minister Shoichi Nakagwa called on Japan and ASEAN to tighten export controls jointly on materials for WMD as an effort to fight against terrorism.[68]

The Asia-Pacific Economic Council (APEC) also has begun to address the link between trade and security. The first major meeting of APEC for 2004 provided encouragment for member nations to sign on to international nonproliferation treaties.[69] In addition, APEC members agreed to a series of joint actions to ensure that key Pacific Rim infrastructure in the areas of trade, finance, and information systems is protected by "Enhancing Secure Trade in the APEC Region (STAR)," which includes calls for greater coordination on container, aviation, and transit security.

While such economic organizations as ASEAN and APEC are by no means the organizational equivalents of the EU, they can provide a framework for the creation of many of the export control norms, best practices and information sharing functions.[70] For example, these organizations could host seminars on transshipment controls involving regional governments and freight forwarding, customs brokers, and the shipping industry—in addition to serving as information sharing platforms on end users of concern. Such services would reduce the institutional costs to national governments while increasing awareness of key export control issues.

Beyond supplying export control resources to and facilitating the coordination of policy of area governments, a regional solution also should be sought regarding informing and assisting industry.[71] Government outreach to industry represents one of the least developed aspects of national export controls in Asia. While Japan's METI, for example, collaborates with a nongovernmental organization, the Center for Information on Security Trade Control, to work with industry in developing compliance programs, other states do not have similar programs. A regional solution also would include ways and means by which to assist regional governmental outreach efforts to industry, an aspect otherwise lacking from ASEAN or APEC agendas.

On the basis of further economic regionalization, a regional solution is the most appropriate means to address the respective export control deficiencies. In spite of that, such an outcome depends entirely on strong leadership and support. The United States has provided a great deal of bilateral export control assistance to many states in the region. For example, the U.S. Department of Commerce recently launched the Transshipment Country Export Control Initiative (TECI).[72] Perhaps more importantly, Japan has been providing such leadership and support for the past decade. Given the accelerated export control developments in China, Beijing should be encouraged to seek broader regional coordination on export control issues. At the 2003 ASEAN summit, for example, China proposed the establishment of a new security mechanism. Under the rubric of the ASEAN Regional Forum (ARF), the organization's mechanism for security discussions, Chinese Foreign Minister Li Zhaoxing proposed forming a conference to increase communication among Asian militaries. In addition, Japan and China hosted their first joint export control seminar in Beijing on March 5, 2004, for Chinese firms.[73]

CONCLUSION: THE FUTURE OF EXPORT CONTROLS IN THE ASIAN REGION

When compared with supplier state export control systems such as the United States and Japan, most states in the region have only the most rudimentary of control systems. That being said, however, regional governments have been making progress on addressing systematic deficiencies on a voluntary and, more importantly, a cooperative basis. To sustain this progress, participating states must understand that export controls are not impediments to trade. On the contrary, they are the prerequisites for ensuring the necessary international and regional stability and technology transfer on which economic development and growth depend.

As Asia develops into a clearly demarcated economic "region," it is confronted by similar export control challenges as those faced in Europe with the advent of the Common Market. As such, a regional system of export control standards and practices emerged as a means to ensure not only economic parity, but also regional and international security. While not necessarily as advanced in terms of regional identity as the European free trade area, the states of Asia could profitably benefit from a regional approach to export control development and coordination.

To help facilitate export control developments in Asia, U.S. leadership and resources are essential. To meet this objective, the United States should pursue the following:

- Provide export control resources and training. Since the early 1990s, the U.S. Government has provided these for the countries of the former Soviet Union. Such assistance is now required in the Asia region. Bilateral export control cooperative programs are now in the offing with countries like Singapore and China. Working with regional nonproliferation leaders like Japan, the United States must expand the scope of its export control programs to include countries with fledgling trade control systems, such as Malaysia.

- Hold China to its nonproliferation commitments. In May 2004, China joined the Nuclear Suppliers Group, thereafter seeking entry into the Missile Technology Control Regime (MTCR). China's recent domestic and international export control developments must be matched against a marked change in behavior. The United States must serve as guarantor that Beijing will adhere to its growing battery of nonproliferation commitments, as Chinese inaction could undermine export control developments made elsewhere in the region.

- Expand Asian involvement in the Proliferation Security Initiative (PSI) and Container Security Initiative (CSI). PSI and CSI are responses to the growing challenge posed by the proliferation of WMD, their delivery systems, and related materials worldwide. Greater Asian participation in both programs is necessary for their collective success.

- Foster and sustain political support. As countries in the region further develop their respective export control capacities—especially China—on-going U.S. support will be critical to achieving this end. While financial and intellectual support is fundamental to this task, political and diplomatic support will be required to ensure that domestic political endorsement for these undertakings remains high.

Above all, the abiding export control challenge for any government is identifying, then striking, the proper balance between trade and security. In this respect, it is critical that export controls are not viewed as impediments to trade. The nexus of trade and security cuts to the heart of the matter in Asia, where national economies depend greatly on trade, as they do on regional and international security. The internal challenge for countries of the Asia region is to develop systems compatible with their political, economic, and security needs while addressing the overall threat posed by the proliferation of WMD.

ENDNOTES

1. Al-Qaeda is alleged to have experimented with procedures for making blister, mustard, nerve, sarin, and VX chemical agents. Furthermore, while some observers point optimistically to the decline in the number of international terrorist incidents during the 1990s as an especially noteworthy and salutary development in the struggle against terrorism, at the same time the proportion of persons killed in terrorist incidents has paradoxically increased. See Bruce Hoffman, "Terrorism and Weapons of Mass Destruction: An Analysis of Trends and Motivations," *RAND Document P-8039*, 1999, pp. 44-50. See also John Parachini, "Putting WMD Terrorism into Perspective," *The Washington Quarterly*, Vol. 26, No. 4, Autumn 2003.

2. As post-Gulf War national and international investigations revealed, Iraq *purchased*—either directly or through front companies—the majority of materials and technologies needed for its various weapons programs. U.S. officials maintained that Iraq, prior to March 2003, accelerated its quest for nuclear weapons and had embarked on a worldwide hunt for materials to make an atomic bomb. Iraq sought to buy thousands of specially designed aluminum tubes, which American officials believe were intended as components of centrifuges to enrich uranium. See Michael Gordon and Judith Miller, "U.S. Says Hussein Intensifies Quest for A-Bomb Parts," *The New York Times*, September 8, 2002. Preliminary reports on Pakistan's role in a worldwide nuclear proliferation network indicate that a wide array of legitimate commercial channels was employed to transfer sensitive goods and technologies. See Kamran Khan, "Pakistanis Exploited Nuclear Network: Iran, Libya Aided Via Black Market, Investigation Finds," *The Washington Post*, January 28, 2004; and David E. Sanger and Raymond Bonner, "A Tale of Nuclear Proliferation: How A Pakistani Built His Network," *The New York Times*, February 12, 2004.

3. *Technology and Security in the 21st Century: U.S. Military Export Control Reform*, Washington, DC: Center for Strategic and International Studies (CSIS), 2001; *Study Group on Enhancing Multilateral Export Controls For U.S. National Security: Final Report*, April 2001; The Henry L. Stimson Center and Defense Science Board Task Force on Globalization and Security, Final Report, Washington, DC: Office of the Under Secretary of Defense for Acquisition and Technology, December 1999.

4. For the purposes of this monograph, "Asia region" is defined as Australia, Brunei, Cambodia, Indonesia, Japan, Laos, Malaysia, Mongolia, Myanmar, Pakistan, People's Republic of China, Democratic People's Republic of Korea, Philippines, Taiwan, Republic of Korea, Singapore, Sri Lanka, Thailand, and Vietnam. India and Pakistan were not included as most scholarship on Asian regionalization does not treat them. Generally, they are treated, in security terms, as a relatively unique dyad. For export control studies on Indian and Pakistan, see Seema Galhaut and Anupam Srivastava, "Curbing Proliferation from Emerging Suppliers: Export Controls in India and Pakistan," *Arms Control Today*, September 2003; and Seema Galhaut, "India," in Michael Beck, Richard Cupitt, Seema Gahlaut,

and Scott Jones, eds., *To Supply or To Deny: Nonproliferation Export Controls in Five Key Countries*, New York: Kluwer, 2003.

5. Asian countries are frequently targets of proliferation acquisition activities. For example, see "Iran Denies Seeking to Buy Missile Technology from Japanese Firm," *Agence France Presse*, June 16, 2003.

6. See Richard Cupitt, "Nonproliferation Export Controls in East Asia," *The Journal of East Asian Affairs*, Vol. 11, No. 2, Summer/Fall 1997, pp. 452-480.

7. See Scott A. Jones, "Current and Future Challenges for Asian Nonproliferation Export Controls," *East Asian Review*, Vol. 15, No. 2, Summer 2003.

8. The literature on what constitutes regionalism or a region is extensive. Not only is it contested, but an important process in Asia has been changing views on, or understandings of, what constitutes the Asian region, for substantive economic and security reasons and for narrower political reasons. An excellent overview is found in Andrew Hurrell, "Explaining the Resurgence of Regionalism in World Politics," *Review of International Studies*, Vol. 21, 1995, pp. 331-358. See also Edward A. Mansfield and Helen V. Milner, eds., *The Political Economy of Regionalism*, New York: Columbia University Press, 1998. An examination of the "regionalist" dynamic in Asia is found in Peter J. Katzenstein, "Regionalism and Asia," *New Political Economy*, Vol. 5, No. 3, 2000, pp. 353-368.

9. World Trade Organization, International Trade Statistics 2002, *http://www.wto.org/english/res_e/statis_e/its202_e/its02_toc_3.htm*.

10. According to the U.S. Customs, over 200 million cargo containers per year move between these ports. *http://www.customs.gov/xp/cgov/newsroom/highlights/csi/*.

11. Trade statistics culled from the World Trade Organization's web site.

12. In 1977, bilateral trade amounted to $77 million. It is now over several billion per year. M. Dutta, *Economic Regionalization in the Asia-Pacific: Challenges to Economic Cooperation*, Cheltenham: Edward Elgar Publishing, 2000. See also Greg Mastel, "WTO Means more than Trade to China," *Journal of Commerce*, April 28, 2000.

13. "New Approaches to Trade and Investment Policies in Asia and the Pacific," United Nations Economic and Social Commission for Asia and the Pacific (UNESCAP), ESCAP Secretariat, Trade and Investment Division, Occasional Papers, 2001, *http://www.unescap.org/itid/publication/chap2_2126.pdf*.

14. Glenn Hook, *et al.*, "Japan and the East Asian Financial Crisis: Patterns, Motivations and Instrumentalization of Japanese Regional Economic Diplomacy," *European Journal of East Asian Studies*, Vol. 1, No. 2, 2002.

15. As a consequence of the 1997 financial crisis, the finance ministers of ASEAN+3 countries (China, Japan, and South Korea) reached agreement on the "Chiang Mai Initiative," which was the first significant regional financing arrangement to enable countries to cope with disruptive capital flows and maintain

exchange rate stability. The Chiang Mai Initiative has contributed to improving exchange rate stability and in doing so may also have contributed to closer regional economic and financial integration. Eiji Ogawa, "Monetary Integration in East Asia," *The Journal of East Asian Affairs*, Vol. 15, No. 2, Fall/Winter 2001, pp. 344-365. See also "Asian Multilateral Institutions and Their Response to the Asian Economic Crisis: The Regional and Global Implications," *The Pacific Review*, Vol. 13, No. 3, 2000, pp. 495-516.

16. Richard Stubbs, "ASEAN Plus Three: Emerging East Asian Regionalism?" *Asian Survey*, Vol. 42, No. 3, 2002.

17. Byeong Hae Sohn, "Regionalization of Trade and Investment in East Asia and Prospects for Further Regional Integration," *Journal of the Asia Pacific Economy*, Vol. 7, No. 2, 2002.

18. "Pipe Dreams," *Economist*, January 20, 2001.

19. Interestingly, these negotiations in the sale and distribution of energy have fostered greater cooperation on issues of naval security. As the Strait of Malacca is among the world's busiest sealanes, China's rising exports and increasing demand for oil have led its navy and its diplomats to pay more attention to the region's shipping lanes and the accessibility of the region's ports. Since 1998, Beijing has stepped up its diplomacy toward old foes, Cambodia and Vietnam, both of which possess key ports. For example, in November 2000 Jiang Zemin made the first visit by a Chinese leader to Phnom Penh in 37 years. One month later, Jiang signed a historic agreement with Vietnam that resolved disputed borders. In return for courting these two Southeast Asian states, Beijing hopes to gain access to Vietnam's Cam Ranh Bay port and Cambodia's Sihanoukville port. China has also boosted naval ties with Thailand and Burma.

20. See Joshua Kurlantczick, "Is East Asia Integrating?" *The Washington Quarterly*, Vol. 24, No. 4, Autumn 2001, pp. 19-28.

21. The regional cooperation and integration literature traditionally has been dominated by neorealist and institutionalist approaches. They have a number of differences, but they also share common assumptions: they focus primarily on cooperation between states, although some institutionalist approaches acknowledge that nonstate actors may facilitate cooperation among nations, and they do not problematize what actually constitutes a *region*. If we acknowledge that the region is best viewed as lived social space, then we need approaches that also highlight regional actors and their political, socioeconomic and sociocultural projects—views absent in the orienting presumptions of both theories. One such approach is Neumann's "region building approach." See Iver B. Neumann, "A Region-Building Approach," in Fredrik Soderbaum and Timothy M. Shaw, eds., *Approaches to the New Regionalism*, London: Palgrave, 2002. See also James J. Hentz and Morten Bøas, eds., *New and Critical Security and Regionalism: Beyond the Nation State*, London: Ashgate, 2003.

22. This high level of military spending was curtailed somewhat by the Asian economic crisis, which resulted in overall reductions in government expenditures

as well as currency depreciation that made some arms imports prohibitively expensive. Still, even though the strong growth in Asian military expenditures slowed, overall expenditures have still not started to decline even in East Asia, which was most affected by the economic crisis. While the volume of arms procurement has been scaled down significantly due to the reduced purchasing power of these governments' currencies, the domestic burden of the military expenditure is not declining.

23. In Southeast Asia, most nations have relatively small military budgets and small armed forces; but here, too, imports or major weapons and military spending are on the rise, contributing to the increased militarization of the Asia-Pacific region.

24. *SIPRI Year Book 2002: Armaments, Disarmaments, and International Security*, Stockholm: SIPRI, 2002.

25. See Joseph Cirincione, "The Asian Nuclear Reaction Chain," *Foreign Policy*, Spring 2000.

26. North Korea began its development of ballistic missiles by reverse-engineering Soviet-made Scud Bs. The Soviet Union, however, did not supply Scud-type missiles to North Korea. In the late 1970s, North Korea acquired a number of Scud Bs from Egypt in return for its assistance to Egypt during the 1973 Yom Kippur War. Seung-Ho Joo, "Military Relations between Russia and North Korea, *The Journal of East Asian Affairs*, Vol. 15, No. 2, Fall/Winter 2001, pp. 297-323.

27. The Democratic People's Republic of Korea (DPRK) also stands accused of exporting nuclear technology to the gas centrifuge enrichment plant in Natanz, Iran. Glenn Kessler, "Iran's Nuclear Program Speeds Ahead," *The Washington Post*, March 10, 2003.

28. Unclassified Report to Congress on the Acquistion of Technology Relating to Weapons of Mass Destruction and Advanced Conventional Munitions, July 1 Through December 31, 2001, Office of the Director of Central Intelligence, *http://www.cia.gov/cia/publications/bian/bian_jan_2003.htm*. In particular, for Washington, the North Korean missile problem has proved to be even more vexing since it also has to take into consideration South Korea's overall response strategies and the fallout from pursuing a regional Theater Missile Defense (TMD) system. In response to North Korea's accelerated missile programs, South Korea has insisted that it should be able to develop medium-range missiles with the capability to hit most targets in North Korea. Although the United States agrees in principle to South Korea's proposal that it should have, in response, the leeway to develop its own missile arsenal with a range up to 300 km, Washington is concerned that such a move could fuel a new arms race in the region. China is keenly concerned about a U.S.-sponsored TMD archipelago running from Taiwan to South Korea. See Don Kirk, "U.S. and Japan to Join in Missile Defense to Meet Pyongyang Threat," *International Herald Tribune*, July 29, 1999; and Andrew Browne, "China Says US Missile Defense Plan 'Last Straw'," *Taiwan Security Research*, March 5, 1999.

29. On February 24, North Korea fired an anti-ship cruise missile into the Sea of Japan, upstaging the inauguration of South Korean President Roh Moo-hyun, who has vowed to push for unconditional reconciliation toward the communist neighbor. Seoul Defense Minister Cho Young-kil said North Korea conducted the missile test several months earlier than scheduled as part of a "brinkmanship tactic" aimed at pressing for two-way security negotiations with the United States. Cho has warned North Korea against further "dangerous" military maneuvers that could bring "serious consequences" to the peninsula, referring to the earlier missile test and the March 2, 2003, interception of a U.S. spy plane by North Korean jet fighters. North Korea reacted angrily to Seoul's warning by saying "irrational acts" would lead to returning inter-Korean relations to a state of confrontation. Howard French, "North Korea Tests a Missile as South Korea Prepares for a New President," *The New York Times*, February 25, 2003.

30. Bertil Lintner, "North Korean Companies and Commercial Activities in Southeast Asia," *Jane's Consultancy*, paper presented at the 11th Asian Export Control Seminar, October 18-20, 2003, Tokyo, Japan.

31. For example, China promised to abide by the Missile Technology Control Regime (MTCR) in 1991-92 and reaffirmed that commitment in an October 4, 1994, statement. Also, China acceded to the Nuclear Nonproliferation Treaty (NPT) on March 9, 1992. China signed the Chemical Weapons Convention (CWC) in January 1993. In November 1995, China issued its first public defense white paper, which focused on arms control and disarmament. On May 11, 1996, the PRC issued a statement promising to make only safeguarded nuclear transfers. China, on July 30, 1996, began a moratorium on nuclear testing and signed the Comprehensive Test Ban Treaty (CTBT) in September 1996 but, like the United States, has not ratified it. On April 25, 1997, China deposited its instrument of ratification of the CWC before it entered into force on April 29, 1997. Premier Li Peng issued new nuclear export control regulations on September 10, 1997. On October 16, 1997, China joined the Zangger Committee on nuclear trade. Finally, China issued regulations on dual-use nuclear exports on June 17, 1998.

32. Director of Central Intelligence (DCI), Unclassified Report to Congress on the Acquisition of Technology Relating to Weapons of Mass Destruction and Advanced Conventional Munitions, July-December 1996 (June 1997), see *http://www.fas.org/irp/cia/product/wmd.htm*. Subsequent reports have noted China's improving nonproliferation policy and behavior. However, problems remain. For instance, in the most recent Report, the DCI observed: "Over the past several years, Beijing improved its nonproliferation posture through commitments to multilateral arms control regimes, promulgation of export controls, and strengthened oversight mechanisms, but the proliferation behavior of Chinese companies remains of great concern." See Unclassified Report to Congress on the Acquisition of Technology Relating to Weapons of Mass Destruction and Advanced Conventional Munitions, 1 January Through 30 June 2003 (*http://www.cia.gov/cia/reports/721_reports/jan_jun2003.htm*).

33. Shirley Kan, "China's Proliferation of Weapons of Mass Destruction and Missiles: Current Policy Issues Updated July 1, 2002," *Issue Briefs for Congress*, Congressional Research Service, The Library of Congress. See also Jing Dong Yuan, "The Evolution of China's Nonproliferation Policy since the 1990s: Progress, Problems, and Prospects," *Journal of Contemporary China*, Vol. 11, No. 31, pp. 209-233; and Yuzo Murayama, "China's Export Control Policy in East Asian Context: Implications from Economic Perspectives," paper presented at the Sixth ISODARCO Beijing Seminar on Arms Control, October 29-November 1, 1998, Shanghai, China.

34. On December 3, 2003, China's State Council published a new *White Paper on Nonproliferation*. In contrast to previous white papers, including the 1995 *White Paper on Arms Control and Disarmament*, this document is low on rhetoric and focuses on documenting recent concrete steps in China's nonproliferation policy. A discussion of China's new export control regulations takes up more than half of the paper. This new *White Paper* gives a clear indication of progress on China's nonproliferation thinking. Although Chinese Premier Wen Jiabao's visit to the United States influenced the timing of the *White Paper's* release, many within China's export control community have pushed for increased transparency on these issues for some time. Chinese export control officials have argued for the last year that their system is improving and that Beijing is taking proliferation issues seriously. By publishing this *White Paper*, Beijing is telling the international nonproliferation community, and particularly the United States, that their efforts are worth noting. A copy of the *White Paper* is available at *http://www.nti.org/db/china/engdocs/nprolwp_03.htm*. See also Evan S. Medeiros and M. Taylor Fravel, "China's New Diplomacy, *Foreign Affairs*, November-December 2003.

35. Mike Narkter, "China Seeks to Join Nuclear Suppliers Group," *Global Security Newswire*, January 27, 2004. In addition, a Statement of Intent was signed in Beijing between the U.S. Department of Energy and the China Atomic Energy Authority (CAEA) on January 12, 2004. The agreement establishes a process for cooperation with each other and for collaborating with the International Atomic Energy Agency (IAEA) on a range of nuclear nonproliferation and security activities. These activities include efforts to strengthen export controls, international nuclear safeguards, physical protection of nuclear materials and facilities, nuclear emergency management, and radioactive source security by setting up information exchanges and training programs. See "Security Cooperation Agreement Signed with U.S.," *Nuclear News*, March 2004.

36. In addition to Jemaah Islamiah, similar groups include the Abu Sayyaf Group and Moro Islamic Liberation Front in the Philippines and the Kumpulan Militan Malaysia in Malaysia.

37. Regarding the emerging trend of radicalized religious groups and WMD use, noted terrorism expert Bruce Hoffman argues that "the growth of religious-inspired terrorism has already contributed to international terrorism's increasing lethality and also that many of the constraints (both self-imposed and technical) that previously prevented terrorist use of WMD are eroding as well. In

this respect, the different characteristics, justifications, and mindsets of religious and quasi-religious—as compared to secular terrorists—suggest that religious-inspired terrorists will be the most likely nonstate perpetrators to use WMD." Bruce Hoffman, "Terrorism and WMD: Some Preliminary Hypotheses," *The Nonproliferaiton Review*, Spring/Summer 1997, pp. 45-53.

38. See Richard Cupitt, S. Grillot, and Y. Murayama, "Determinants of Nonproliferation Export Controls: A Membership-Fee Explanation," *The Nonproliferation Review*, Vol. 8, No. 2, Summer 2001, pp. 69-80.

39. Japan joined COCOM in 1952 and adopted Import Certificate/Delivery Verification (IC/DV) system that was similar to the ones adopted by other COCOM countries and adhered strictly to COCOM rules, such as implementing controls over re-exports and end-user checks. In 2001, Japan enacted catch-all legislation.

40. An enhanced application of ODA with respect to export control assistance recently was initiated. Tokyo is in the process of ranking Asian countries' export control policies and differentiating them in terms of ODA support. The ranking system will rate aid-receiving countries into four groups according to their export control development: 1) systems roughly similar to Japan's; 2) developing systems; 3) primitive systems; and 4) countries without functioning systems. The government will calibrate its export control assistance accordingly. See "Japan to Tighten Export Controls to Asia to Prevent Arms Proliferation," BBC Monitoring Asia-Pacific, published in *Yomiuri Shimbun*, January 5, 2004.

41. Security Export Control Council, Industrial Structure Committee, Ministry of International Trade and Industry, *The Future of Security Export Controls*, Tokyo, March 25, 1993, pp. 1-3. Based on this recommendation, Japan launched its "Asian Export Control Initiative" to promote and coordinate the adoption of nonproliferation export controls in the region. The Japanese Industrial Structure Council reported that "[r]einforcing export controls . . . to achieve world peace is an area in which it is most appropriate for Japan to play a role commensurate with its status as a major economic power" and that "appropriate export controls on dual-use items" are important in meeting the proliferation threat.

42. COCOM, established in 1949, was used by the major Western industrial powers to impose restrictions on the transfer of militarily useful technology to the Soviet bloc. At the time of its elimination, COCOM was by far the most comprehensive export control mechanism dealing with "dual-use" technologies—items which have both commercial and military applications. Dual-use transfers are of particular concern in stemming the spread of capabilities for the production of the full spectrum of weapons systems, from small arms to major conventional systems to weapons of mass destruction.

43. "Japan, H.K., Singapore Plan WMD Export Curbs," *Daily Yomiuri*, January 8, 2004.

44. Jason Leow, "China's Weapons Sales Rules Could Be Double-Edged Sword," *The Straits Times*, August 30, 2002.

45. Chuang Peck Ming, "Bill Tightens Control Over Exports of Strategic Goods," *The Business Times Singapore*, November 26, 2002.

46. Throughout the 1990s, Libya had been able to purchase hundreds of millions of dollars' worth of nuclear parts, including advanced centrifuges designed in Pakistan, from a firm in Malaysia, with a free-trade zone in Dubai serving as the main shipping point. It was a new development in an old arms race: Malaysia, a high-tech nation with no indigenous nuclear ambitions, was retailing sophisticated nuclear gear, based on designs made available by Pakistani nuclear scientist A. Q. Khan. Seymour Hersh, "Why is Washington Going Easy on Pakistan's Nuclear Black Marketeers?" *The New Yorker*, March 8, 2004. See also David Crawford, "Supply Chain: How the Pakistani Nuclear Ring Managed to Skirt Export Laws," *The Wall Street Journal*, March 23, 2004.

47. Center for Information on Strategic Technologies, "Questionnaire on Export Control Systems in Asian Countries and Regions," Tokyo, Japan, March 2003. The authorities surveyed included Brunei, Cambodia, China, Hong Kong, Indonesia, Japan, Laos, Macao, Malaysia, Mongolia, Myanmar, the Philippines, South Korea, Taiwan, Thailand, Singapore, and Vietnam. The data that follow come from this survey.

48. Surveys conducted since 1999 indicate little development in controls over strategic technologies, especially regarding controls over so-called "intangible transfers of technology."

49. Richard Sako and Louis Lambert, "The Changing Face of Export Controls: How the War on Terrorism is Affecting Corporate Export Compliance Obligations," *Legal Media*, July 2002, *http://www.legalmedia.net*.

50. Yuan, Jing-Dong, "The Future of Export Controls: Developing New Strategies for Nonproliferation," *International Politics*, Vol. 39, No. 2, June 2002.

51. See Joseph Cirincione, "Global Trends," in J. Cirincione, *Deadly Arsenals: Tracking Weapons of Mass Destruction*, Washington DC: Carnegie Endowment for International Peace, 2002, pp. 3-25.

52. At its annual meeting in Paris on June 6, 2002, the Australia Group agreed to adopt a new set of formal guidelines on licensing exports of sensitive items. Two of the most important provisions in the new set of guidelines are the no-undercut and catch-all provisions. The catch-all provision directs Australia Group members to license exports of materials that could be used to develop biological or chemical weapons, even if the specific item is not identified on the group's control lists. Exporters must also alert authorities if they are aware that unlisted items are meant for a biological or chemical weapons program. This is the first time that an export control regime has agreed to include a catch-all clause in its public guidelines.

53. Similarly, China has indicated that it will apply special "scrutiny and caution" on missile-related exports to those countries developing nuclear-capable ballistic missiles, even if the items do not appear on the control list.

54. For a comprehensive study of the Chinese export control system, see Richard T. Cupitt, "China," in M. Beck, R. Cupitt, S. Galhaut, and S. Jones, eds., *To Supply or To Deny: Nonproliferation Export Controls in Five Key Countries*, New York: Kluwer Law International, 2003.

55. Karen Bhatia, Deputy Undersecretary for Industry and Security, Remarks at the Regional Forum on Transshipment Controls, December 12, 2002, Bangkok, Thailand, *http://www.bxa.doc.gov/press/2002/Bhatia@BanqkokForum.html*.

56. For example, John Bolton, Undersecretary of State for Arms Control and International Security, noted that "The whole administration is focusing more on transshipment countries," especially those in Asia. William Neal, "Export Controls: U.S. Pushes Out the Borders," *National Journal*, December 30, 2002.

57. Following a recent investigation, the South Korean Ministry of Commerce, Industry, and Energy concluded that a company it identified only by its initial (D) shipped four balancing machines to a Middle Eastern country, according to officials. In December, the International Atomic Energy Agency (IAEA) found the Korean-made machines during nuclear inspections of Libya. Balancing machines, used to balance centrifuges, are listed as strategic materials requiring government permission for export by the NSG. It is the second time a South Korean company has been charged with exporting NSG-controlled strategic materials. In October, the government filed a complaint against a local company (identified as W) on similar charges. "ROK Government Accuses Domestic Firm of Exporting WMD-Related Equipment to Libya," *Seoul Yonhap*, February 11, 2004.

58. A telecomparator is a precision manufacturing device that is accurate to the 0.2 micrometer.

59. According to Ryokosha spokesman Teruhito Koizumi, it had known the machines sold to a South Korean agent were going to China, but the company was assured that the proper applications to export the telecomparators would be processed. The spokesman also said the company realized it was a mistake to send personnel to offer assistance to the end user. See F. J. Khergamvala, "Japan Detects Export of Nuke Products to China," *The Hindu*, February 9, 1999.

60. Statement of Richard Mercier, Executive Director for Investigative Programs, Office of Investigations, U.S. Customs Service, Before the U.S.-China Commission, January 17, 2002, *http://usinfo.state.gov/regional/ea/uschina/mercier.htm*.

61. William New, "Export Controls: United States Pushing Out the Borders," *National Journal*, December 30, 2002.

62. Malaysia's involvement, albeit inadvertent, in supplying Libya with nuclear enrichment components is a case in point. See "U.S. Envoy Urges Malaysia to Improve Its Export Rules," *Associated Press*, March 2, 2004.

63. The processes of regional integration in non-European parts of the world have not yet been studied meticulously. There are basically two main reasons for this. First, the existing literature on regional integration generally has focused on the process of European integration. Second, the studies on the processes of

integration in non-European parts of the world largely have been conducted in isolation from the contributions of the studies on European integration. An excellent study is Christopher Dent and David Huang, *Northeast Asian Regionalism—Learning from the European Experiences*, London: Routledge, 2002.

64. See Burkhart Schmitt, "A Common European Export Policy for Defense and Dual-Use Items?" Occasional Paper 25, Institute for Security Studies, Western European Union, May 2001; Panos Koutrakos, "The Reform of Common Rules on Exports of Dual-Use Goods under the Law of the European Union, *European Journal of Law Reform*, Vol. 2, No. 2, Spring 2000; *Report to the European Parliament and the Council on the application of regulation (EC) 3381/94 setting up a Community system of export controls regarding dual-use goods* (Com, 98), Brussels, May 1998; and *Proposal for a Council Regulation setting up a Community regime for the control of exports of dual-use goods and technology*, COM(1998), 98/0162, ACC, prepared by the Commission.

65. Muthiah Alagappa, ed., *Asian Security Practice: Material and Ideational Influences*, Stanford: Stanford University Press, 1998.

66. Nobuo Okawara and Peter J. Katzenstein, "Japan and Asian-Pacific Security: Regionalization, Entrenched Bilateralism and Incipient Multilateralism," *The Pacific Review*, Vol. 14, No. 2, 2001, pp. 165–194. See also Bertil Lintner, "North Korean Companies and Commercial Activities in Southeast Asia," *Jane's Consultancy*, paper presented at the 11th Asian Export Control Seminar, October 18-20, 2003, Tokyo, Japan.

67. A somewhat critical, but nevertheless informative, view of regional anti-terrorism cooperation is found in David Jones and Mike Smith, "From *Konfrontasi* to *Disintegrasi*: ASEAN and the Rise of Islamism in Southeast Asia," *Studies in Conflict & Terrorism*, Fall 2002, pp. 343-356.

68. "Japan, ASEAN to Meet on WMD Proliferation Export Controls," *Kyodo News Service*, February 6, 2004.

69. On the "fungibility" of regional organizations to adopt new issue areas, see Mark Beeson, "Reshaping Regional Institutions: APEC and the IMF in East Asia," *The Pacific Review*, Vol. 12, No. 1, 1999, pp. 1-29.

70. Jürgen Haacke, "Collective Foreign and Security Policy: The Emergence of an ASEANized Regional Order in East Asia?" London School of Economics Department of International Relations, International Studies Association Annual Meeting, Minneapolis, MN, March 1998.

71. The growing sophistication of WMD-related technologies and expansion of global trade have taxed the control and monitoring capabilities of national export control systems. In addition, the inclusion of the catch-all clause in national export control systems worldwide has accelerated the necessity of developing industry outreach programs, as the obligation of the exporter now extends beyond published control lists. Consequently, export control strategies now emphasize the enhanced responsibility of industry in preventing the spread of WMD-related goods and technologies.

72. The announcement of the TECI program was made at the Southeast Asian Conference on Trade Security in Bangkok, Thailand, in December 2002. The TECI program works alongside another U.S. export control program, the Container Security Initiative (CSI). The initiative is designed to enhance security of the sea cargo container. One of the core elements of CSI involves placing U.S. Customs inspectors at major foreign seaports, such as Singapore and Hong Kong, to pre-screen cargo containers before they are shipped to America. U.S. Customs officials, working with their foreign counterparts, will be in a position to detect potential WMD in U.S.-bound containers at these foreign ports.

73. The seminar was attended by division chief-level officials from ministries and agencies of the two governments including the Ministry of Economy, Trade and Industry (METI) and people from about 100 companies in China. Export managers from Japanese electric appliance manufacturers served as lecturers. They taught how to monitor products that may possibly be used for producing nuclear weapons, biological and chemical weapons, and missiles. "Japan, PRC To Cooperate in Export Control To Prevent WMD Proliferation," *Sankei Shimbun*, March 5, 2004.

APPENDIX I

ACQUISITION CASE STUDY: NORTH KOREAN COMPANIES AND COMMERCIAL ACTIVITIES IN SOUTHEAST ASIA[1]

In line with directives issued by North Korea's Ministry of the People's Armed Forces and Bureau 39 of the Korean Workers' Party, North Korean embassies and trading companies in Southeast Asia have been mobilized to raise hard currency for the state and the party. Next to the Middle East, where North Korea is making vast amounts of money from its trade in ballistic missiles and missile technology, Southeast Asia is the most important place for the North Koreans to do business. In brief, the North Koreans are raising money and conducting their businesses in the region in the following five different ways.

1. DPRK Embassies.

The embassies themselves import duty free cars, liquor, perfume, and cigarettes, which they sell on the black market. This is the practice, especially in Thailand, whose laws are not always as forcefully enforced as is the case in, for instance, Singapore and Malaysia. Money raised in this manner most probably is used to finance the operations of the embassies, as they have been told to be self-sufficient, and they do not receive enough funding from Pyongyang. In early 2001, fake U.S.$100 notes also turned up in Bangkok. One of the North Korean diplomats there was caught red-handed trying to deposit the forgeries in a local bank.

2. DPRK Trading Companies.

Connected with the embassies, but not part of them, is a maze of supposedly privately-owned trading companies. In Thailand, for instance, a company which is officially registered as Kosun Import-Export and permitted to trade in rice, rubber, paper, tapioca, and clothing, also owns an eight-story building in Bangkok and is involved in property. It rents out flats and office space in the building it owns. Money earned in this manner is used to finance the embassy in Bangkok, and to support the regime in Pyongyang.

3. DPRK Defense Technology Transfer.

Other North Korean-trading companies in Southeast Asia—mainly in Thailand, Singapore, and Hong Kong—have been set up with the specific purpose of obtaining technology for North Korea's defense industries. In the past, much of this technology could be obtained in Japan through the Chosen Soren, but stricter controls by Japanese authorities have prompted the North Koreans to look elsewhere for electronic goods produced by Japan and other countries. Since this activity is of a more clandestine nature than more ordinary trading carried out by companies such as Kosun, they carefully disguise the location and nature of the company in question. One such company in Bangkok is Kotha Trading (Korea-Thailand). It has one North Korean shareholder—the managing director of the company—who carries a diplomatic passport from North Korea. The others are "sleeping" Thai partners. According to the Thai companies' registry, it is supposed to be dealing in ceramics. But first, the address at which it is officially registered—an office block not far from the North Korean embassy in Bangkok—is not where its actual office is located. That is more than two kilometers away in another office block where it shares facilities with three or four Thai electronics companies. Kotha Trading is connected with a world-wide network of North Korean trading companies that are procuring spare parts and components for North Korea's defense industries, including its ballistic missile programs. Goods are shipped either directly to North Korea, or indirectly through China. Similar companies also operate in Hong Kong and Singapore. There are about a dozen North Korean Trading Companies in Hong Kong, and about the same number in Singapore.

4. Proxy Companies.

Because of restrictions in Japan, Japanese goods destined for North Korea are often rerouted through countries such as Thailand. In November last year, for instance, a company in Tokyo called Meishin, which is owned by local businessmen connected with the Chosen Soren, first attempted to export three power-control devices to North Korea. But when the Japanese authorities refused to issue an export license, the three devices were disguised as something else and sent to Bangkok. The recipient in Bangkok was not a North Korean-owned company—which would have been too suspicious—but a perfectly legitimate Thai company, Loxley Pacific, one of Thailand's leading telecommunications firms. But Loxley also has an investment in North Korea where it is installing a mobile phone system.

In this case, the goods never reached North Korea. They were seized by customs in Hong Kong, where the ship stopped on its way to Bangkok, because the documents accompanying the power-control devices were not in order. In converted use, these power-control devices can be used in the production of WMD. Loxley, however, claimed that "The electricity situation is poor in North Korea . . . they need stabilizers to avoid hurting their household appliances." A less than likely explanation, but it shows how the North Koreans are also using third-party middlemen to get the goods they require to North Korea.

5. Direct Procurement and Acquisition.

The fifth area of activity is even more intriguing as it is characterized by direct procurement and acquisition of controlled materials. In Thailand, a North Korean-owned company, Wolmyongsan Progress Joint Venture, was engaged for years in mining activities near the Burmese border in western Thailand. It is unclear what minerals it was mining, and if it was to sell them to make money, or use them in North Korea's defense industries. But Thai sources suspect they were looking for uranium and other strategic minerals. Wolmyongsan is no longer active in Thailand, but another North Korean mining company has been detected in Laos, a communist-run state with close relations to North Korea. The company, Chosun-Lao Seok Hoisa (in Korean: "the Korea-Laos Stone Company"), is said to be mining for tin at four locations around Sup Sitae near Hinboun in Khammouane province. However, it may also be looking for other more strategic minerals. In recent months, North Korean mining specialists have also been spotted at a location 7 kms south of Taunggyi in the Shan State of Burma. The cooperation with Burma is new, as relations between the two countries were broken after North Korean agents placed a powerful bomb in Rangoon in 1983, killing several visiting South Korean government ministers.

ENDNOTE

1. Study is derived wholly from Bertil Lintner, "North Korean Companies and Commercial Activities in Southeast Asia," *Jane's Consultancy*, paper presented at the 11th Asian Export Control Seminar, October 18-20, 2003, Tokyo, Japan. Please do not cite without author's approval.

☆U.S. GOVERNMENT PRINTING OFFICE: 2004- 704 –049/00031